LIONS

Published by Creative Education, Inc., 123 South Broad Street, Mankato, Minnesota 56001

Library of Congress Cataloging-in-Publication Data

Wexo, John Bonnett.
Lions / by John Bonnett Wexo.
p.   cm. — (Zoobooks)
Summary: Discusses lions and their habits and habitats and includes several lion-related activities.
ISBN 0-88682-422-2
1. Lions—Juvenile literature. [1. Lions.] I. Title. II. Series: Zoo books (Mankato, Minn.)
QL737.C23W49   1991   599.74'428—dc20   91-11811 CIP AC

LIONS

Series Created by
John Bonnett Wexo

Editorial Consultants
Ann Elwood
Jackie Estrada

Zoological Consultant
Charles R. Schroeder, D.V.M.
Director Emeritus
San Diego Zoo &
San Diego Wild Animal Park

Scientific Consultants
Michael R. Worley, D.V.M.
Zoological Society of San Diego

Christopher A. Shaw
Eric Scott
George C. Page Museum

Art Credits

All paintings by Richard Orr. **Activities Art** by Pamela Morehouse.

Photographic Credits

Cover: © Tom O'Brian (After Image); **Pages Six and Seven:** R.S. Virdee (Grant Heilman); **Page Eight:** Jean Vertut; **Page Ten:** Y. Arthus-Bertrand (Peter Arnold, Inc.); **Page Eleven:** Peter Davey (Bruce Coleman, Ltd.); **Page Twelve:** Lecz Lemoine (Natural History Photographic Agency); **Page Thirteen:** Jeff Foot (Tom Stack & Associates); **Pages Fourteen and Fifteen:** M. P. Kahl (Bruce Coleman, Inc.); **Page Sixteen:** R.H. Armstrong (Animals Animals); **Page Seventeen: Center,** William and Marcia Levy (Photo Researchers); **Bottom,** G.D. Dodge and D.R. Thompson; **Page Eighteen: Center,** Ernest Manewal (Shostal Associates); **Lower Center,** Peter Davey (Bruce Coleman, Inc.); **Page Nineteen: Left,** Ron Kimball; **Right,** Stephen J. Krasemann (Peter Arnold, Inc.); **Pages Twenty and Twenty-one:** Peter Johnson (Natural History Photographic Agency).

Our Thanks To: Annalisa Berta (San Diego State University); Rachel Oberlander; Michaele M. Robinson (San Diego Zoo); Linda A. Rill; Oliver Ryder (San Diego Zoo); Joe Selig.

Contents

*L*ions are among the most admired animals on earth. Their strength and beauty, combined with their bold natures, have fascinated people for ages. In fact, the lion has often been called the "king of the beasts." And when you see a big male lion, with its magnificent mane and proud walk, it's easy to understand why. Lions really *do* look like kings.

But lions don't always lead the easy lives of kings. They often need to work hard to survive. Lions are meat eaters, or *carnivores*, so they must hunt other animals for food. And sometimes prey is hard to find. When food is scarce, a lion may go for days without eating.

Lions are members of the big cat family, which includes tigers, leopards, and jaguars. The main difference between the big cats and all other cats is that big cats can roar but cannot purr. Other cats can purr but cannot roar.

The lion is one of the biggest cats in the world. Only the Siberian tiger is larger. A male lion may be 9 to 10 feet long (3 meters) and can weigh 500 pounds (227 kilograms) or more. Female lions are smaller. The average female is 7 to 8 feet long (2½ meters) and weighs 270 to 350 pounds (140 kilograms).

Lions are different from most other cats in that they live in groups. They hunt together, guard their territory together, and raise their young together. Lions that live in groups can catch more food than a single lion can. And they can protect themselves better. Also, lions that are born into groups have a large family to care for them.

There are two different kinds, or *subspecies*, of lions—the *African* and the *Asiatic*. Most of the lions in the world today are African lions. These animals live on the grassy plains of Africa. The few Asiatic lions that remain live on a small wildlife preserve in India. As you will see, there were once many other kinds of lions in the world—but all of these are now *extinct*.

Both African and Asiatic lions are *endangered*. This is because people are taking away their homes, or *habitats*. The human population in Africa and Asia is rapidly growing, and people are turning more and more land into farms and ranches. This means that the lions have less food to eat—and so it is harder for them to live.

Fortunately, wildlife organizations throughout the world are working hard to save the lions' habitats. And governments in both Africa and India have set aside special land where lions can live in safety.

Lions sometimes climb high up into trees to rest on their branches and escape the biting insects below.

*L*ions are found today in only a few parts of the world. The map on these pages shows that they live in small areas of Africa and in a very small section of India. But in the past, lions lived *all over the world,* on every continent except Antarctica and Australia. (The green areas on the map show where lions used to live. The orange areas show where they live today.)

Ten thousand years ago, there were lions in North America and even in South America. Only two thousand years ago, there were still lions in Europe. And two hundred years ago, lions roamed in many parts of Asia and all over Africa.

What happened to all of these lions? We aren't sure why lions died out thousands of years ago. But we do know that they are dying out now as a result of human actions.

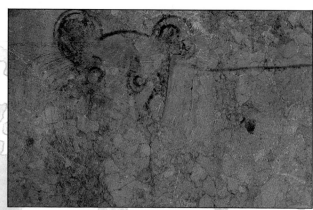

Prehistoric people in Europe painted this lion on the wall of a cave more than 15,000 years ago. At that time, there were still hundreds of thousands of lions in Europe. Today, there are none.

NORTH AMERICA

The last lions in North America probably died out about 10,000 years ago.

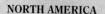

NORTH AMERICAN
Panthera atrox
(Extinct)

The lions of North America were giants. They preyed on bison, camels, horses, and other large animals that lived in North America in the past.

SOUTH AMERICA

North American lions were almost 12 feet long (3½ meters). Their heads were 1½ feet long (½ meter), and they had teeth that were 2½ inches long (6½ centimeters).

EUROPEAN CAVE LION
Panthera leo spelaea
(Extinct)

AFRICAN LION

European lions were huge animals, like the North American lions. They were larger than the modern African lion.

EUROPE

ASIA

ASIATIC LION
Panthera leo persica
(Living)

AFRICA

AFRICAN LION
Panthera leo
(Living)

At one time, there were millions of lions all over Africa. Now there are fewer than 200 thousand. In most places, lions died out because wild land was converted into farms and ranches. As a result, wild prey became scarce, and lions could not find enough to eat. Hunters also killed many lions.

In the past, hundreds of thousands of Asiatic lions were found in the Middle East and Asia. Now *only 180 survive*. Like the African lions, they have suffered from the destruction of wild lands and hunting.

*T*he body of a lion is made for catching prey. Most of the time, lions try to get very close to their prey before they attack it. Then they make a big leap and grab the prey.

To help them get close without being seen, lions have golden-brown coats that blend in with the land around them. And to help them leap, they have strong muscles in their legs. A lion can leap *35 feet (10½ meters)* through the air in a single jump.

Lions do most of their hunting at night, so they have wonderful hearing and eyesight to help them find prey in the dark. Their hearing is so sharp, they can hear prey that is more than a mile away. The eyes of lions are the biggest of any meat-eating animal. Like the eyes of other cats, they are specially made for seeing at night.

Long, sharp teeth—called *canines*—and strong claws are used to grab prey.

Lions can turn their ears from side to side to catch sounds coming from almost any direction. When a lion is moving through tall grass, it may not always be able to see its prey—but it can always *hear* it.

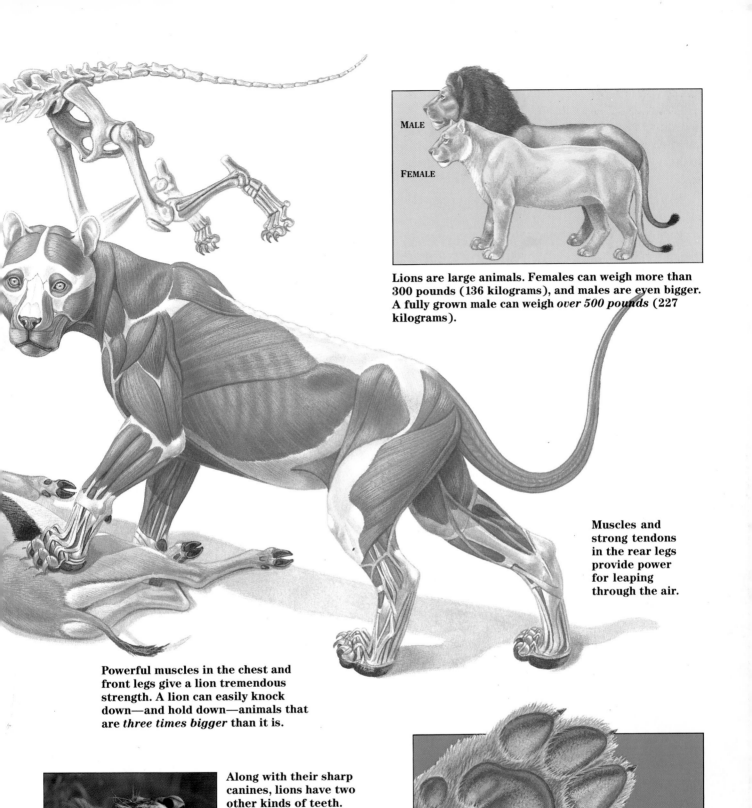

Lions are large animals. Females can weigh more than 300 pounds (136 kilograms), and males are even bigger. A fully grown male can weigh *over 500 pounds* (227 kilograms).

MALE

FEMALE

Muscles and strong tendons in the rear legs provide power for leaping through the air.

Powerful muscles in the chest and front legs give a lion tremendous strength. A lion can easily knock down—and hold down—animals that are *three times bigger* than it is.

Along with their sharp canines, lions have two other kinds of teeth. *Large teeth* in the back of the mouth are used to cut up large pieces of meat. *Small teeth* in the front of the mouth can nip small pieces of meat off bones. A special *tongue* has a very rough surface for scraping the last tiny bits of meat off bones.

To help them sneak up on prey, lions have rubbery pads on the bottoms of their feet. Like sneakers, the pads soften the sound of each step.

A family of lions is called a *pride*. Lions are the *only* cats that live in large family groups, and the group is very important in a lion's life. For one thing, a group of lions is much better at catching food than a single lion. This means that all members of a pride are likely to eat better and stay healthier. All of the lions in a pride also work together to raise the young and keep them safe.

A pride of lions contains between 4 and 30 animals. This includes several females and their young, and one or more males. Each pride has its own *territory*, or area in which it lives. The male lions guard the territory and protect it from outsiders. But as you will see below, a male lion can only stay with a pride if he is *stronger* than outside males who try to take over the group.

The lions in a pride are very sociable. They *enjoy* being together, and can be friendly and affectionate. When they meet, they often say "hello" by rubbing their heads together.

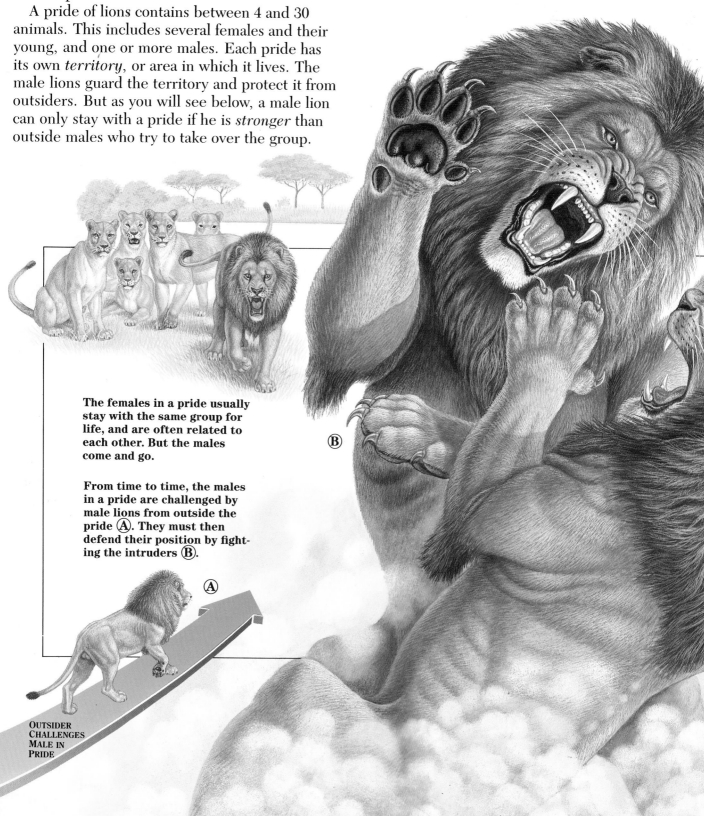

The females in a pride usually stay with the same group for life, and are often related to each other. But the males come and go.

From time to time, the males in a pride are challenged by male lions from outside the pride (A). They must then defend their position by fighting the intruders (B).

Ⓐ

Ⓑ

OUTSIDER CHALLENGES MALE IN PRIDE

When separated, lions roar to let each other know where they are. A roar can be heard up to *5 miles* (8 kilometers) away. Females often call their cubs by roaring.

Like people, lions use the expressions on their faces to show each other how they feel. Can you tell what these lions are feeling? (The answers are printed upside down below each picture.)

AFRAID

ANNOYED

ANGRY

The females in a pride usually do the hunting— but when the hunt is over, the males often drive the females away from the meat and take "the lion's share" for themselves. The females and cubs eat the rest, and there is usually plenty for everybody.

(D)
DEFEATED MALE LEAVES

If the outsider wins, he joins the pride (C). The defeated male is forced to leave (D). He may go off to live by himself, or with a group of other males.

(C)

NEW MALE
JOINS PRIDE

Lions can be very lazy. When their stomachs are full, they may spend 20 hours every day just lying around, resting and sleeping. They often snuggle close together.

Lions often work together when they hunt. By doing this, they increase their chances of getting food. A lion that hunts alone may have a hard time catching prey.

Most of the hunting is done by a team of females. They divide the job among them, with each female doing *part* of the work to catch the prey. As you will see below, some of the females scare prey animals and make them run—while other females lie in ambush to grab the fleeing animals.

The extra strength of a male is sometimes needed to bring down *larger* animals, like wildebeest or buffalo. And larger animals are the best prey, because they provide *more meat*.

To start the hunt, the lion team divides into two groups. One group circles around to get ahead of the prey Ⓐ.

When the first group is in position, the other group shows itself and scares the prey Ⓑ.

The frightened prey stampedes— and runs right into the first group of lions Ⓒ.

When they can, lions get their food by taking it away from other animals. This is often easier than hunting. In some parts of Africa, much of the food that lions eat is taken away from hyenas.

When food is really scarce, lions will eat almost *anything* they can find—including snakes, locusts, termites, peanuts, fruit, and rotten wood.

No matter how good a lion is at hunting, it misses more prey than it catches. Sometimes lions will go for days without eating.

If lions can't find enough of their regular prey, they will eat smaller animals like hares and tortoises— and even porcupines.

Baby lions are called cubs. And like most baby animals, they need lots of loving care. A lion cub is totally helpless at birth. It is blind and can barely crawl. And it weighs less than 5 pounds (2 kilograms).

Cubs are born in groups called *litters*. Usually, there are three cubs in a litter. But sometimes there are as many as five. For the first few weeks of their lives, the cubs stay hidden in a safe place away from the pride. Then their mother brings them out to join the "family."

In a pride, all of the females help take care of the cubs. When one mother is away hunting, the other lions feed and watch over her young. But sometimes, all of the adults join the hunt. Then the cubs are hidden in the tall grass or among the rocks.

A mother lion carries her babies in her mouth—just like a mother house cat. To keep predators from finding the cubs, she moves them to a new hiding place every few days.

A cub is born with dark spots all over its body, which fade after a few months. Some people think that the spots may make it harder for predators to see the cubs when they are hidden.

When cubs grow older, they often lie out in the open waiting for their mother to return from hunting.

Like kittens, cubs will pounce on anything that moves. By playing in this way, cubs learn the hunting skills they will need when they grow up.

Male lions are very patient with cubs. It's amazing how a big male will let a cub tug at his mane or bat at the black tuft on the end of his tail.

If beautiful lions like this one are to survive in
the wild, we must find ways to save their habitats
from destruction. Find out how *you* can help.
Write to: World Wildlife Fund, 1250 24th St., N.W.,
Washington, DC 20037.

21

Now that you've read all about lions, have some fun! The activities on these pages will help you see for yourself how much you've learned.

- Lions are meat eaters, or ■■■■■■■■■■ .

- Most of the lions in the world today are found in ■■■■■■ .

- When separated, lions ■■■■ to let each other know where they are.

- Lions are ■■■■■■■■■■ because people are taking away their homes.

Lion Word Puzzle

Complete each of the following sentences about lions by listing the missing word on a piece of paper. (The number of boxes shows the number of letters in the missing word.) Then look at the first letter in each word you wrote to discover a secret word.

Answers

Endangered
Roar
Africa
Carnivores

Are You a Good Stalker?

Lions hunt by *stalking*, or sneaking up on, their prey and surprising it before it can run away. How good are *you* at stalking prey? You can test yourself. First, decide what your prey will be—perhaps your *cat* or *dog* or a *brother* or *sister* (no fair picking your pet turtle!). You will need to choose a time and place when you can hide—maybe when you are playing outside. Then try to sneak up on your prey. Look for good places to hide, such as behind bushes. And remember that lions flatten themselves to the ground when they are stalking. See how close you can get before your prey notices you. **If you can touch your prey before he or she knows you're there, you are a successful stalker!**

Make a Lioness Mask!

You'll need: heavy construction paper, crayons or marking pens, and 1 or 2 long rubber bands.

1 On a piece of construction paper, draw a big circle slightly larger than the size of your face. Now draw a small circle (a) for the mouth and 2 smaller circles (b) for the ears.

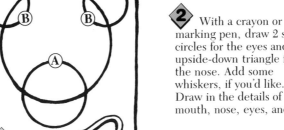

3 Use scissors to cut out the mask.

4 With the point of a pencil, very carefully punch a small hole in both sides of the mask. Cut a long rubber band into one piece, and thread the ends through the holes. You may need to use 2 rubber bands tied together. To hold the rubber band in place, tie a knot at each end.

2 With a crayon or marking pen, draw 2 small circles for the eyes and an upside-down triangle for the nose. Add some whiskers, if you'd like. Draw in the details of the mouth, nose, eyes, and fur.

5 Your mask is finished! Put it on and wear it to stalk prey or to play lion games!

LION WORD SCRAMBLE

Can you unscramble these words?

Looking for food:
T G U I H N N

Where lions like to hide:
S A R S G

A family of lions:
E I R P D

Target of a meat-eater:
Y R P E

Area that a pride of lions defends:
R E Y R R T O I T

Answers:
HUNTING, GRASS, PRIDE, PREY, TERRITORY

How many lions can you find in this picture?

If you can find 5 or more lions, you're a lion cub.

If you can find 10 or more, you're a member of the pride.

If you can find 15 or more, you're the pride leader!

LION QUIZ

1. Which lions do most of the hunting in prides?
2. How far can a lion leap?
3. The last lions in North America probably died out about _____ years ago.
4. What is the only country outside of Africa where lions live in the wild?
5. How many cubs are usually born in a litter?
6. Female lions call their cubs by _____.

Answers to Quicky Quiz
1. Females
2. 35 feet (10½ meters)
3. 10,000
4. India
5. 2 or 3
6. Roaring

23

Index